D1005979

Presented to _____Eileen_____

From _____Judy_____ '93_____

BY HELEN STEINER RICE

HELEN STEINER RICE

Sunshine of Joy

Fleming H. Revell Company • Old Tappan, New Jersey

The poems in this volume were previously included in
the book *Gifts From the Heart*.

Illustrations Copyright ©1988 by Steffi Karen Rubin
Text Copyright ©1968 by the Fleming H. Revell Company,
1988 by the Helen Steiner Rice Foundation

Published by the Fleming H. Revell Company
Old Tappan, New Jersey 07675
Printed in the United States of America

CONTENTS

Whatever the celebration, whatever the day, whatever the event, whatever the occasion, Helen Steiner Rice possessed the ability to express the appropriate feeling for that particular moment in time.

A happening became happier, a sentiment more sentimental, a memory more memorable because of her deep sensitivity to put into understandable language the emotion being experienced. Her positive attitude, her concern for others, and her love of God are identifiable threads woven into her life, her works... and even her death.

Prior to her passing, she established the HELEN STEINER RICE FOUNDATION, a nonprofit corporation whose purpose is to award grants to worthy charitable programs that aid the elderly, the needy, and the poor. In her lifetime, these were the individuals about whom Mrs. Rice was greatly concerned.

Royalties from the sale of this book will add to the financial capabilities of the HELEN STEINER RICE FOUNDATION, thus making possible additional grants. In the four years of its existence, the foundation has presented seventy-four grants, ranging from three thousand to fifteen thousand dollars each, to various, qualified, worthwhile, and charitable programs. Because of her foresight, her caring, and her deep convictions, Helen Steiner Rice continues to touch a countless number of lives. Thank you for your assistance in helping to keep Helen's dream alive.

Virginia J. Ruehlmann, Administrator
THE HELEN STEINER RICE FOUNDATION

My Thanks!

People everywhere in life
        from every walk and station,
From every town and city
        and every state and nation
Have given me so many things
        intangible and dear,
I couldn't begin to count them all
        or even make them clear. . .
I only know I owe so much
        to people everywhere
And when I put my thoughts in verse
        it's just a way to share
The musings of a thankful heart,
        a heart much like your own,
For nothing that I think or write
        is mine and mine alone . . .
So if you found some beauty
        in any word or line,
It's just "your soul's reflection"
        in "proximity with mine."

HELEN STEINER RICE

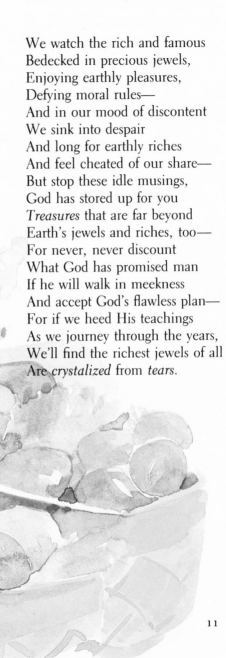

God's Jewels

We watch the rich and famous
Bedecked in precious jewels,
Enjoying earthly pleasures,
Defying moral rules—
And in our mood of discontent
We sink into despair
And long for earthly riches
And feel cheated of our share—
But stop these idle musings,
God has stored up for you
Treasures that are far beyond
Earth's jewels and riches, too—
For never, never discount
What God has promised man
If he will walk in meekness
And accept God's flawless plan—
For if we heed His teachings
As we journey through the years,
We'll find the richest jewels of all
Are *crystalized* from *tears*.

The Gift of Lasting Love

Love is much more than a tender caress
     and more than bright hours of gay happiness,
For a lasting love is made up of sharing
     both hours that are "joyous" and also "despairing". . .
It's made up of patience and deep understanding
     and never of selfish and stubborn demanding,
It's made up of climbing the steep hills together
     and facing with courage life's stormiest weather . . .
And nothing on earth or in heaven can part
     a love that has grown to be part of the heart,
And just like the sun and the stars and the sea,
     this love will go on through eternity—
For "true love" lives on when earthly things die,
     for it's part of the spirit that soars to the "sky."

God, Grant Me the Glory of Thy Gift

God, widen my vision so I may see
      the afflictions You have sent to me—
Not as a cross too heavy to bear
      that weighs me down in gloomy despair—
Not as something to hate and depise
      but a gift of love sent in disguise—
Something to draw me closer to You
      to teach me the patience and forbearance, too—
Something to show me more clearly the way
      to serve You and love You more every day—
Something priceless and precious and rare
      that will keep me forever safe in Thy care
Aware of the spiritual strength that is mine
      if my selfish, small will is lost in Thine!

The Gift of God's Love

All over the world at this season,
Expectant hands reach to receive
Gifts that are lavishly fashioned,
The finest that man can conceive.
For, purchased and given at Christmas
Are luxuries we long to possess,
Given as favors and tokens
To try in some way to express
That strange, indefinable feeling
Which is part of this glad time of year
When streets are crowded with shoppers
And the air resounds with good cheer.
But back of each tinsel-tied package
Exchanged at this gift-giving season,
Unrecognized often by many,
Lies a deeper, more meaningful reason.
For, born in a manger at Christmas
As a gift from the Father above,
An infant whose name was called Jesus
Brought mankind the gift of God's love.
And the gifts that we give have no purpose
Unless God is a part of the giving,
And unless we make Christmas a pattern
To be followed in everyday living.

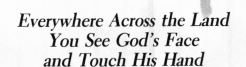

Everywhere Across the Land
You See God's Face
and Touch His Hand

Each time you look up in the sky
Or watch the fluffy clouds drift by,
Or feel the sunshine warm and bright,
Or watch the dark night turn to light,
Or hear a bluebird gayly sing,
Or see the winter turn to spring,
Or stop to pick a daffodil,
Or gather violets on some hill,
Or touch a leaf or see a tree,
It's all *God* whispering, *"This is Me
And I am Faith and I am Light
And in Me there shall be no night."*

So Many Reasons
to Love the Lord

Thank You, God, for little things
      that come unexpectedly
To brighten up a dreary day
      that dawned so dismally—
Thank You, God, for sending
      a happy thought my way
To blot out my depression
      on a disappointing day—
Thank You, God, for brushing
      the dark clouds from my mind
And leaving only sunshine
      and joy of heart behind.
Oh, God, the list is endless
      of things to thank You for
But I take them all for granted
      and unconsciously ignore
That *everything* I think or do,
      each movement that I make,
Each measured rhythmic heartbeat,
      each breath of life I take
Is something You have given me
      for which there is no way
For me in all my smallness
      to in any way repay.

16

God Is Never
Beyond Our Reach

No one ever sought the Father
And found *He* was not *there*,
And no burden is too heavy
To be lightened by a prayer,
No problem is too intricate
And no sorrow that we face
Is too deep and devastating
To be softened by His grace,
No trials and tribulations
Are beyond what we can bear
If we share them with *Our Father*
As we talk to *Him* in prayer—
And men of every color,
Every race and every creed
Have but to seek the Father
In their deepest hour of need—
God asks for no credentials,
He accepts us with our flaws,
He is kind and understanding
And He welcomes us because
We are His erring children
And He loves us every one,
And He freely and completely
Forgives all that we have done,
Asking only if we're ready
To follow *where He leads*—
Content that in His wisdom
He will answer all our needs.

Unaware, We Pass "Him" By

On life's busy thoroughfares
We meet with *angels* unawares—
But we are too busy to listen or hear,
Too busy to sense that God is near,
Too busy to stop and recognize
The grief that lies in another's eyes,
Too busy to offer to help or share,
Too busy to sympathize or care,
Too busy to do the *good things* we should,
Telling ourselves we would if we could.
But life is too swift and the pace is too great
And we dare not pause for we might be late
For our next appointment which means so much,
We are willing to brush off the Savior's touch,
And we tell ourselves there will come a day
We will have more time to pause on our way.
But before we know it "life's sun has set"
And we've passed the Saviour but never met,
For hurrying along life's thoroughfare
We passed Him by and remained unaware
That within the *very sight of our eye,*
Unnoticed, the Son of God passed by.

Anywhere Is a Place of Prayer
If God Is There

I have prayed on my knees in the morning,
I have prayed as I walked along,
I have prayed in the silence and darkness
And I've prayed to the tune of a song—
I have prayed in the midst of triumph
And I've prayed when I suffered defeat,
And I have prayed on the sands of the seashore
Where the waves of the ocean beat—
I have prayed in a velvet-hushed forest
Where the quietness calmed my fears,
I have prayed through suffering and heartache
When my eyes were blinded with tears—
I have prayed in churches and chapels,
Cathedrals and synagogues, too,
But often I've had the feeling
That my prayers were not getting through,
And I realized then that our Father
Is not really concerned *where* we pray
Or impressed by our manner of worship
Or the eloquent words that we say—
He is only concerned with our feelings,
And He looks deep into our heart
And hears the "cry of our soul's deep need"
That no words could ever impart.
So it isn't the prayer that's expressive
Or offered in some special spot,
It's the sincere plea of a sinner
And God can tell whether or not
We honestly seek His forgiveness
And earnestly mean what we say,
And then and then only He answers
The prayer that we fervently pray.

Where Can We Find Him?

Where can we find *the Holy One?*
Where can we see *His Only Son?*
The Wise Men asked, and we're asking still,
Where can we find this Man of Good Will?

Is He far away in some distant place,
Ruling unseen from His throne of grace?
Is there nothing on earth that man can see
To give him proof of *eternity?*
It's true we have never looked on His face,
But His likeness shines forth from every place,
For *the hand of God* is everywhere
Along life's busy thoroughfare.
And His presence can be felt and seen
Right in the midst of our daily routine,
The things we touch and see and feel
Are what make God so very real.
The silent stars in timeless skies,
The wonderment in children's eyes,
The gossamer wings of a hummingbird,
The joy that comes from a kindly word,
The autumn haze, the breath of spring,
The chirping song the crickets sing,
A rosebud in a slender vase,
A smile upon a friendly face,
In everything both great and small
We see *the hand of God in all,*
And every day, somewhere, someplace,
We see *the likeness of His Face.*
For who can watch a new day's birth
Or touch the warm, life-giving earth,
Or feel the softness of the breeze
Or look at skies through lacy trees
And say they've never seen His face
Or looked upon His throne of grace!

In Hours of Discouragement
God Is Our Encouragement

Sometimes we feel uncertain
And unsure of everything,
Afraid to make decisions,
Dreading what the day will bring.
We keep wishing it were possible
To dispel all fear and doubt
And to understand more readily
Just what life is all about.
God has given us the answers
Which too often go unheeded,
But if we search His promises
We'll find everything that's needed
To lift our faltering spirits
And renew our courage, too,
For there's absolutely nothing
Too much for God to do.
For the Lord is our salvation
And our strength in every fight,
Our redeemer and protector,
Our eternal guiding light.
He has promised to sustain us,
He's our refuge from all harms,
And underneath this refuge
Are the everlasting arms.
So cast your burden on Him,
Seek His counsel when distressed,
And go to Him for comfort
When you're lonely and oppressed.
For God is our encouragement
In trouble and in trials,
And in suffering and in sorrow
He will turn our tears to smiles.

Love: God's Gift Divine

Love is enduring
And patient and kind,
It judges all things
With the heart not the mind,
And love can transform
The most commonplace
Into beauty and splendor
And sweetness and grace.
For love is unselfish,
Giving more than it takes,
And no matter what happens
Love never forsakes,
It's faithful and trusting
And always believing,
Guileless and honest
And never deceiving.
Yes, love is beyond
What man can define,
For love is immortal
And God's gift is divine!

The Priceless Gift

The priceless gift of life is love,
For with the help of God above
Love can change the human race
And make this world a better place.
For love dissolves all hate and fear
And makes our vision bright and clear
So we can see and rise above
Our pettiness on "wings of love."

A Friend Is a Gift of God

Among the great and glorious gifts
      our heavenly Father sends
Is the gift of understanding
      that we find in loving friends.
For in this world of trouble
      that is filled with anxious care
Everybody needs a friend
      with whom they're free to share
The little secret heartaches
      that lay heavy on their mind,
Not just a mere acquaintance
      but someone who's "just our kind."
For, somehow, in the generous heart
      of loving, faithful friends
The good God in His charity
      and wisdom always sends
A sense of understanding
      and the power of perception
And mixes these fine qualities
      with kindness and affection,
So when we need some sympathy
      or a friendly hand to touch,
Or an ear that listens tenderly
      and speaks words that mean so much,
We seek our true and trusted friend
      in the knowledge that we'll find
A heart that's sympathetic
      and an understanding mind.
And often just without a word
      there seems to be a union
Of thoughts and kindred feelings
      for God gives true friends communion.

The Gift of Friendship

Friendship is a priceless gift
That cannot be bought or sold,
But its value is far greater
Than a mountain made of gold.
For gold is cold and lifeless,
It can neither see nor hear,
And in the time of trouble
It is powerless to cheer.
It has no ears to listen,
No heart to understand,
It cannot bring you comfort
Or reach out a helping hand.
So when you ask God for a Gift,
Be thankful if He sends
Not diamonds, pearls, or riches,
But the love of real true friends.

Blessings in Disguise
Are Difficult to Recognize

God sends His "little angels"
        in many forms and guises,
They come as lovely miracles
        that God alone devises.
For He does nothing without purpose,
        everything's a perfect plan
To fulfill in bounteous measure
        all He ever promised man.
For every "little angel"
        with a body bent and broken,
Or a little mind retarded
        or little words unspoken,
Is just God's way of trying
        to reach and touch the hand
Of all who do not know Him
        and cannot understand
That often through an angel
        whose "wings will never fly"
The Lord is pointing out the way
        to His eternal sky
Where there will be no handicaps
        of body, soul, or mind,
And where all limitations
        will be dropped and left behind.
So accept these "little angels"
        as gifts from God above
And thank Him for this lesson
        in *faith* and *hope* and *love.*

Before You Can Dry Another's Tears—
You Too Must Weep!

Let me not live a life that's free
From *"the things"* that draw me close to *Thee*—
For how can I ever hope to heal
The wounds of others I do not feel—
If my eyes are dry and I never weep,
How do I know when the hurt is deep—
If my heart is cold and it never bleeds,
How can I tell what my brother needs—
For when ears are deaf to the beggar's plea
And we close our eyes and refuse to see,
And we steel our hearts and harden our minds,
And we count it a weakness whenever we're kind,
We are no longer following *the Father's Way*
Or seeking His guidance from day to day—
For, without "crosses to carry" and "burdens to bear,"
We dance through a life that is frothy and fair,
And "chasing the rainbow" we have no desire
For "roads that are rough" and "realms that are higher"—
So spare me no heartache or sorrow, dear Lord,
For the heart that is hurt reaps the richest reward,
And God enters the heart that is broken with sorrow
As He opens the door to a *brighter tomorrow*,
For only through tears can we recognize
The suffering that lies in another's eyes.

Trouble Is a Stepping-stone to Growth

Trouble is something no one can escape,
Everyone has it in some form or shape—
Some people hide it way down deep inside,
Some people bear it with gallant-like pride,
Some people worry and complain of their lot,
Some people covet what they haven't got,
While others rebel and become bitter and old
With hopes that are dead and hearts that are cold . . .
But the wise man accepts whatever God sends,
Willing to yield like a storm-tossed tree bends,
Knowing that God never makes a mistake,
So whatever He sends they are willing to take—
For trouble is part and parcel of life
And no man can grow without trouble and strife,
And the steep hills ahead and high mountain peaks
Afford man at last the peace that he seeks—
So blest are the people who learn to accept
The trouble men try to escape and reject,
For in *our acceptance*
        we're given great grace
And courage and faith and the strength to face
The daily troubles that come to us all
So we may learn to stand "straight and tall"—
For the grandeur of life is born of defeat
For in overcoming we make life complete.

When Trouble Comes
and Things Go Wrong!

Let us go quietly to God
       when troubles come to us,
Let us never stop to whimper
       or complain and fret and fuss,
Let us hide "our thorns" in "roses"
       and our sighs in "golden song"
And our "crosses" in a "crown of smiles"
       whenever things go wrong.
For no one can really help us
       as our troubles we bemoan,
For *comfort, help,* and *inner peace*
       must come from God alone.
So do not tell your neighbor,
       your companion, or your friend
In the hope that they can help you
       bring your troubles to an end,
For they, too, have their problems,
       they are burdened just like you,
So *take your cross to Jesus*
       and *He will see you through.*
And waste no time in crying
       on the shoulder of a friend
But go directly to the Lord
       for on Him you can depend.
For there's absolutely *nothing*
       that His mighty hand can't do
And He never is too busy
       to help and comfort you.

God Knows Best

Our Father knows what's best for us,
So why should we complain—
We always want sunshine
But He knows there must be rain.
We love the sound of laughter
And the merriment of cheer,
But our hearts would lose their tenderness
If we never shed a tear.
Our Father tests us often
With suffering and with sorrow.
He tests us, not to punish us,
But to help us meet *tomorrow*.
For growing trees are strengthened
When they withstand the storm,
And the sharp cut of the chisel
Gives the marble grace and form.
God never hurts us needlessly,
And He never wastes our pain,
For every loss He sends to us
Is followed by rich gain.
And when we count the blessings
That God has so freely sent,
We will find no cause for murmuring
And no time to lament.
For Our Father loves His children,
And to Him all things are plain,
So He never sends us *pleasure*
When the *soul's deep need is pain*.
So whenever we are troubled,
And when everything goes wrong,
It is just God working in us
To make *our spirit strong*.

"This Too Will Pass Away"

If I can endure for this minute
Whatever is happening to me,
No matter how heavy my heart is
Or how "dark" the moment may be—
If I can remain calm and quiet
With all my world crashing about me,
Secure in the knowledge God loves me
When everyone else seems to doubt me—
If I can but keep on believing
What I know in my heart to be true,
That "darkness will fade with the morning"
And that *this will pass away, too*—
Then nothing in life can defeat me
For as long as this knowledge remains
I can suffer whatever is happening
For I know God will break "all the chains"
That are binding me tight in *"the darkness"*
And trying to fill me with fear—
For there is *no night without dawning*
And I know that *"my morning"* is near.

Quit Supposin'

Don't start your day by supposin'
    that trouble is just ahead,
It's better to stop supposin'
    and start with a prayer instead,
And make it a prayer of *Thanksgiving*
    for the wonderful things God has wrought
Like the beautiful sunrise and sunset,
    "God's Gifts" that are free
    and not bought.
For what is the use of supposin'
    the dire things that could happen to you
And worry about some misfortune
    that seldom if ever comes true.
But instead of just idle supposin'
    step forward to meet each new day
Secure in the knowledge God's near you
    to lead you each step of the way.
For supposin' the worst things will happen
    only helps to make them come true
And you darken the bright, happy moments
    that the dear Lord has given to you.
So if you desire to be happy
    and get rid of the *"misery of dread"*
Just give up *"supposin' the worst things"*
    and look for *"the best things"* instead.

Never Borrow Sorrow
From Tomorrow

Deal only with the present,
Never step into tomorrow,
For God asks us just to trust Him
And to never borrow sorrow.
For the future is not ours to know
And it may never be,
So let us live and give our best
And give it lavishly.
For to meet tomorrow's troubles
Before they are even ours
Is to anticipate the Saviour
And to doubt His all-wise powers.
So let us be content to solve
Our problems one by one,
Asking nothing of tomorrow
Except *"Thy will be done."*

A Sure Way to a Happy Day

Happiness is something
    we create in our mind,
It's not something you search for
    and so seldom find.
It's just waking up
    and beginning the day
By counting our blessings
    and kneeling to pray.
It's giving up thoughts
    that breed discontent
And accepting what comes
    as a "gift heaven-sent."
It's giving up wishing
    for things we have not
And making the best of
    whatever we've got.
It's knowing that life
    is determined for us,
And pursuing our tasks
    without fret, fume, or fuss.
For it's by completing
    what God gives us to do
That we find real contentment
    and happiness, too.

For One Who Gives
So Much to Others

It's not the things that can be bought
        that are life's richest treasure.
It's just the little heart gifts
        that money cannot measure . . .
A cheerful smile, a friendly word,
        a sympathetic nod
Are priceless little treasures
        from the storehouse of our God . . .
They are the things that can't be bought
        with silver or with gold,
For thoughtfulness and kindness
        and love are never sold . . .
They are the priceless things in life
        for which no one can pay,
And the giver finds rich recompense
        in *giving them away*.
And who on earth gives more away
        and does more good for others
Than understanding, kind, and wise
        and selfless, loving *Mothers*
Who ask no more than just the joy
        of helping those they love
To find in life the happiness
        that they are dreaming of.

No Prayer Goes Unheard

Often we pause and wonder,
When we kneel down to pray,
Can God really hear
The prayers that we say.
But if we keep praying
And talking to *Him*,
He'll brighten the soul
That was clouded and dim,
And as we continue
Our burden seems lighter,
Our sorrow is softened
And our outlook is brighter.
For though we feel helpless
And alone when we start,
Our prayer is the key
That opens the heart.
And as our heart opens
The dear Lord comes in
And the prayer that we felt
We could never begin
Is so easy to say
For the Lord understands
And gives us new strength
By the touch of His hands.

Prayers Can't Be Answered Unless
They Are Prayed

Life without purpose
          is barren indeed—
There can't be a harvest
          unless you plant seed,
There can't be attainment
          unless there's a goal,
And man's but a robot
          unless there's a soul.
If we send no ships out,
          no ships will come in,
And unless there's a contest,
          nobody can win.
For games can't be won
          unless they are played.
And *prayers* can't be *answered*
          unless they are *prayed.*
So whatever is wrong
          with your life today,
You'll find a solution
          if you kneel down and pray.
Not just for pleasure,
          enjoyment, and health,
Not just for honors
          and prestige and wealth,
But *pray for a purpose*
          to make life worth living,
And *pray for the joy*
          of unselfish giving,
For *great is your gladness*
          and rich your reward
When you make your *life's purpose*
          the choice of the Lord.

37

Daily Prayers Dissolve Your Cares

I meet God in the morning
And go with Him through the day,
Then in the stillness of the night
Before sleep comes I pray
That God will just "take over"
All the problems I couldn't solve
And in the peacefulness of sleep
My cares will all dissolve,
So when I open up my eyes
To greet another day
I'll find myself renewed in strength
And there'll open up a way
To meet what seemed impossible
For me to solve alone
And once again I'll be assured
I am never *on my own.*
For if we try to stand alone
We are weak and we will fall,
For God is always *greatest*
When we're helpless, lost, and small,
And no day is unmeetable
If on rising our first thought
Is to thank God for the blessings
That His loving care has brought . . .
For there can be no failures
Or hopeless, unsaved sinners
If we enlist the help of God
Who makes all losers winners.
So meet Him in the morning
And go with Him through the day
And thank Him for His guidance
Each evening when you pray,
And if you follow faithfully
This daily way to pray
You will never in your lifetime
Face another "hopeless day."

Prayers Are the Stairs to God

Prayers are the stairs
We must climb every day,
If we would reach God
There is no other way,
For we learn to know God
When we meet Him in prayer
And ask Him to lighten
Our burden of care.
So start in the morning
And, though the way's steep,
Climb ever upward
Till your eyes close in sleep.
For prayers are the stairs
That lead to the Lord,
And to meet Him in prayer
Is the climber's reward.

God's Love

God's love is like an island
In life's ocean vast and wide—
A peaceful, quiet shelter
From the restless, rising tide.

God's love is like an anchor
When the angry billows roll—
A mooring in the storms of life,
A stronghold for the soul.

God's love is like a fortress
And we seek protection there
When the waves of tribulation
Seem to drown us in despair.

God's love is like a harbor
Where our souls can find sweet rest
From the struggle and the tension
Of life's fast and futile quest.

God's love is like a beacon
Burning bright with faith and prayer
And through the changing scenes of life
We can find a haven there!

The Magic of Love

Love is like *magic*
And it always will be,
For love still remains
Life's sweet mystery!

Love works in ways
That are wondrous and strange
And there's nothing in life
That love cannot change!

Love can transform
The most commonplace
Into beauty and splendor
And sweetness and grace!

Love is unselfish,
Understanding, and kind,
For it sees with its heart
And not with its mind!

Love is the answer
That everyone seeks—
Love is the language
That every heart speaks—

Love can't be bought,
It is priceless and free,
Love like pure magic
Is a sweet mystery!

41

God, Grant Us Hope
and Faith and Love

Hope for a world
          grown cynically cold,
Hungry for power
          and greedy for gold.

Faith to believe
          when within and without
There's a nameless fear
          in a world of doubt.

Love that is bigger
          than race or creed,
To cover the world
          and fulfill each need.

God, grant these gifts
Of faith, hope, and love—
Three things this world
Has so little of.
For only these gifts
From our Father above
Can turn man's sins
From hatred to love!

Warm Our Hearts With Thy Love

Oh, God, who made the summer
    and warmed the earth with beauty,
Warm our hearts with gratitude
    and devotion to our duty,
For in this age of violence,
    rebellion, and defiance
We've forgotten the true meaning
    of "dependable reliance."
We have lost our sense of duty
    and our sense of values, too,
And what was once unsanctioned,
    no longer is taboo,
Our standards have been lowered
    and we resist all discipline,
And our vision has been narrowed
    and blinded to all sin.
Oh, put the summer brightness
    in our closed, unseeing eyes
So in the careworn faces
    that we pass we'll recognize
The heartbreak and the loneliness,
    the trouble and despair
That a word of understanding
    would make easier to bear.
Oh, God, look down on our cold hearts
    and warm them with Your love,
And grant us Your forgiveness
    which we're so unworthy of.

In the Garden of Gethsemane

Before the dawn of Easter
    There came Gethsamane,
Before the Resurrection
    There were hours of agony.
For there can be no crown of stars
    Without a cross to bear,
And there is no salvation
    Without *faith* and *love* and *prayer*,
And when we take our needs to God
    Let us pray as did His Son
That dark night in Gethsemane—
    "Thy Will, not mine, be done."

"Why Should He Die for Such as I"

In everything both great and small
We see the hand of God in all,
And in the miracles of Spring
When *everywhere* in *everything*
His handiwork is all around
And every lovely sight and sound
Proclaims the God of earth and sky
I ask myself *"Just who am I"*
That God should send His only Son
That my salvation would be won
Upon a *cross* by a sinless man
To bring fulfillment to God's Plan—
For Jesus suffered, bled, and died
That sinners might be sanctified,
And to grant God's children *such as I*
Eternal life in that *home* on *high*.

My God Is No Stranger

I've never seen God,
    but I know how I feel,
It's people like *you*
    who make *Him* "*so real.*"
My God is no stranger,
    He's friendly and gay
And *He* doesn't ask me
    to weep when I pray.
It seems that I pass *Him*
    so often each day,
In the faces of people
    I meet on the way.
He's the stars in the heaven,
    a smile on some face
A leaf on a tree
    or a rose in a vase.
He's winter and autumn
    and summer and spring,
In short, *God is every*
    real, wonderful thing.
I wish I might meet *Him*
    much more than I do,
I would if there were
    more people like you.

Widen My Vision

God open my eyes
    so I may see
And feel Your presence
    close to me.
Give me strength
    for my stumbling feet
As I battle the crowd
    on life's busy street,
And widen the vision
    of my unseeing eyes
So in passing faces
    I'll recognize
Not just a stranger,
    unloved and unknown,
But a friend with a heart
    that is much like my own.
Give me perception
    to make me aware
That scattered profusely
    on life's thoroughfare
Are the best *gifts of God*
    that we daily pass by
As we look at the world
    with an *unseeing eye.*

"I Know That My Redeemer Liveth"

They asked me how I know it's true
That the Saviour lived and died
And if I believe the story
That the Lord was crucified.
And I have so many answers
To prove His Holy Being,
Answers that are everywhere
Within the realm of seeing.
The leaves that fell in autumn
And were buried in the sod
Now budding on the tree boughs
To lift their arms to God,
The flowers that were covered
And entombed beneath the snow
Pushing through the "darkness"
To bid the spring "hello,"
On every side great nature
Retells the Easter story
So who am I to question
"the Resurrection Glory"?

"I Am the Light of the World"

Oh, Father, up in heaven,
  We have wandered far away
From Jesus Christ, Our Saviour,
  Who arose on Easter Day.
And the promise of salvation
  That God gave us when Christ died
We have often vaguely questioned,
  Even doubted and denied.
We've forgotten why You sent us
  Jesus Christ Your Only Son,
And in arrogance and ignorance—
  It's *our Will*, not *Thine, be done* . . .
Oh, shed *Thy Light* upon us
  As Easter dawns this year,
And may we feel *the presence*
  Of the *Risen Saviour* near.
And, God, in Thy great wisdom,
  Lead us in the way that's right,
And may *"the darkness"* of this world
  Be conquered by *"Thy Light."*

More of Thee . . . Less of Me

Take me and break me and make me, dear God,
Just what you want me to be.
Give me the strength to accept what you send
And eyes with the vision to see
All the small arrogant ways that I have
And the vain little things that I do,
Make me aware that I'm often concerned
More with *myself* than with *You*,
Uncover before me my weakness and greed
And help me to search deep inside
So I may discover how easy it is
To be selfishly lost in my pride.
And then in Thy goodness and mercy
Look down on this weak, erring one
And tell me that I am forgiven
For all I've so willfully done,
And teach me to humbly start following
The path that the dear Saviour trod
So I'll find at the end of life's journey
"A *home in the city of God.*"

God, Give Us "Drive" but Keep Us From Being "Driven"

There's a difference between "drive" and "driven"—
The one is selfish the other God-given.
For the "driven man" has but one goal,
Just worldly wealth and not "riches of soul."
And daily he's spurred on to reach and attain
A higher position, more profit and gain,
Ambition and wealth become his great need
As daily he's "driven" by avarice and greed.
But most blessed are they who use their "drive"
To work with zeal so all men may survive,
For while they forfeit great personal gain
Their work and their zeal are never in vain.
For they contribute to the whole human race
And we cannot survive without growing in grace,
So help us, dear God, to choose between
The "driving force" that rules our routine
So we may make our purpose and goal
Not power and wealth but the growth of our soul.
And give us *strength* and *drive* and *desire*
To raise our standards and ethics higher
So all of us and not *just a few*
May live on earth . . . *as You want us to.*

The Way to God

If my days were untroubled
    and my heart always light
Would I seek that fair land
    where there is no night?
If I never grew weary
    with the weight of my load
Would I search for God's Peace
    at the end of the road?
If I never knew sickness
    and never felt pain
Would I reach for a hand
    to help and sustain?
If I walked not with sorrow
    and lived without loss
Would my soul seek sweet solace
    at the foot of the cross?
If all I desired was mine
    day by day
Would I kneel before God
    and earnestly pray?
If God sent no "Winter"
    to freeze me with fear
Would I yearn for the warmth
    of "Spring" every year?
I ask myself this
    and the answer is plain—
If my life were all pleasure
    and I never knew pain
I'd seek God less often
    and need Him much less,
For God's sought more often
    in times of distress,
And no one knows God
    or sees Him as plain
As those who have met His
    on "the pathway of pain."

53

The World Would Be a Nicer Place If We Traveled at a Slower Pace

Amid stresses and strains
much too many to mention,
And pressure-packed days
filled with turmoil and tension,
We seldom have time
to be "friendly or kind"
For we're harassed and hurried
and always behind—
And while we've more "gadgets"
and "buttons to press"
Making leisure hours greater
and laboring hours less,
And our standards of living
they claim have improved
and "repressed inhibitions"
have been freed and removed,
It seems all this progress
and growth are for naught,
For daily we see a world more distraught—
So what does it matter
if man reaches his goal
"And gains the whole world but loses his soul"—
For what have we won
if in gaining this end
We've been much too busy
to be kind to a friend,
And what is there left to make the heart sing
When life is a cold and mechanical thing
And we are but puppets
of controlled automation
Instead of "joint heirs"
to "God's gift of Creation."

Faith Is a Mighty Fortress

We stand once more at the end of the year
With mixed emotions of *hope and fear*,
Hope for *the peace* we long have sought,
Fear that *our hopes* will come to naught.
Unwilling to trust in the *Father's Will*,
We count on our logic and shallow skill
And, in our arrogance and pride,
Man is no longer satisfied
To place his confidence and love
With *childlike faith* in God above.
But tiny hands and tousled heads
That kneel in prayer by little beds
Are closer to the dear Lord's heart
And of His Kingdom more a part
Than we who search and never find
The answers to our questioning mind,
For faith in things we cannot see
Requires a child's simplicity.
Oh, Father, grant once more to men
A simple *childlike faith* again,
Forgetting *color, race,* and *creed*
And seeing only the heart's deep need.
For *faith* alone can save man's soul
And lead him to a *higher goal,*
For there's but one unfailing course—
We win by *faith* and *not* by *force.*

A Prayer for Patience

God, teach me to be patient
Teach me to go slow
Teach me how to wait on You
When my way I do not know
Teach me sweet forbearance
When things do not go right
So I remain unruffled
When others grow uptight
Teach me how to quiet
My racing, rising heart
So I may hear the answer
You are trying to impart
Teach me to *let go*, dear God,
And pray undisturbed until
My heart is filled with inner peace
And I learn to know *Your* will!

Time Is a Gift of God

We stand once more
on the threshold
of a shining and unblemished year,
Untouched yet by *time* and *frustration*,
unclouded by *failure* and *fear* . . .
How will we use the days of this year
and the *time* God has placed in our hands,
Will we waste the minutes
and squander the hours,
leaving "no prints behind in time's sands" . . .
Will we vainly complain
that *life* is *so swift*,
that we haven't the *time to do good*,
Our days are too crowded,
our hours are too short
to do *all the good things* we should . . .
We say we would pray
if we just had the time,
and be kind to all those in need,
But we live in a world
of *planned progress*
and our national password is *speed* . . .
God, grant us the grace
as another year starts
to use all the hours of our days,
Not for our own selfish interests
and our own willful, often-wrong ways . . .
But teach us
to *take time for praying*
and to find time
for *listening to You*
So each day is spent
well and wisely
doing *what You most want us to do.*

57

The Praying Hands

The *"Praying Hands"* are much, much more
than just a work of art,
They are the "soul's creation"
of a deeply thankful heart—
They are a *Priceless Masterpiece*
that love alone could paint,
And they reveal the selflessness
of an unheralded saint—
These hands so scarred and toilworn,
tell the story of a man
Who sacrificed his talent
in accordance with God's Plan—
For in God's Plan are many things
man cannot understand,
But we must trust God's judgment
and be guided by His hand—
Sometimes He asks us to give up
our dreams of happiness,
Sometimes we must forego our hopes
of fortune and success—
Not all of us can triumph
or rise to heights of fame,
And many times *what should be ours*,
goes to *another name*—
But he who makes a sacrifice,
so another may succeed,
Is indeed a true disciple
of our blessed Saviour's creed—
For when we "give ourselves away"
in sacrifice and love,
We are "laying up rich treasures"
in God's kingdom up above—   .

And hidden in gnarled, toilworn hands
    is the truest *art of living*,
Achieved alone by those who've learned
    the *"victory of giving"*—
For any sacrifice on earth,
    made in the dear Lord's name,
Assures the giver of a place
    in *Heaven's Hall of Fame*—
And who can say with certainty
    Where the greatest talent lies,
    Or who will be the greatest
    in our heavenly Father's eyes!

The Peace of Meditation

So we may know God better
And feel His quiet power,
Let us daily keep in silence
A *meditation hour.*
For to understand God's greatness
And to use His gifts each day
The soul must learn to meet Him
In a meditative way.
For our Father tells His children
That if they would know His will
They must seek Him in the silence
When all is calm and still.
For nature's greatest forces
Are found in quiet things
Like softly falling snowflakes
Drifting down on angels' wings,
Or petals dropping soundlessly
From a lovely full-blown rose,
So God comes closest to us
When our souls are in repose.
So let us plan with prayerful care
To always allocate
A certain portion of each day
To be still and meditate.
For when everything is quiet
And we're lost in meditation,
Our soul is then preparing
For a deeper dedication
That will make it wholly possible
To quietly endure
The violent world around us
For in God we are secure.

The Joy of Unselfish Giving

Time is not measured
    by the years that you live
But by the deeds that you do
    and the joy that you give—
And each day as it comes
    brings a chance to each one
To love to the fullest,
    leaving nothing undone
That would brighten the life
    or lighten the load
Of some weary traveler
    lost on life's road—
So what does it matter
    how long we may live
If as long as we live
    we unselfishly give.

Give Lavishly! Live Abundantly!

The more you give, the more you get—
The more you laugh, the less you fret—
The more you do *unselfishly,*
The more you live *abundantly* . . .

The more of everything you share,
The more you'll always have to spare—
The more you love, the more you'll find
That life is good and friends are kind . . .

For only *what we give away,*
Enriches us from day to day.

Every Day Is a Reason for Giving— and Giving Is the Key to Living!

So let us give "ourselves" away
Not just today but every day . . .
And remember a kind and thoughtful deed
Or a hand outstretched in time of need
Is the rarest of gifts, for it is a part
Not of the purse but a loving heart—
And he who gives of himself will find
True joy of heart and peace of mind.

63

The Seasons of the Soul

Why am I cast down
     and despondently sad
When I long to be happy
     and joyous and glad?
Why is my heart heavy
     with unfathomable weight
As I try to escape
     this soul-saddened state?
I ask myself often—
     "What makes life this way,
Why is the song silenced
     in the heart that was gay?"
and then with God's help
     it all becomes clear,
The *soul* has its *seasons*
     just the same as the year—
I too must pass through
     life's autumn of dying,
A desolate period
     of heart-hurt and crying,
Followed by winter
     in whose frostbitten hand
My heart is as frozen
     as the snow-covered land—
Yes, man too must pass
     through the seasons God sends,
Content in the knowledge
     that everything ends,

And, oh, what a blessing
    to know there are reasons
And to find that our soul
    must, too, have its seasons—
Bounteous seasons
    and *barren ones*, too,
Times for rejoicing
    and times to be blue,
But meeting these seasons
    of dark desolation
With strength that is born
    of anticipation
That comes from knowing
    that "autumn-time sadness"
Will surely be followed
    by a "springtime of gladness."

Finding Faith in a Flower

Sometimes when faith is running low
And I cannot fathom why things are so . . .
I walk alone among the flowers I grow
And learn the "answers" to all I would know!
For among my flowers I have come to see
Life's miracle and its mystery . . .
And standing in silence and reverie
My faith comes flooding back to me!

Not by the Years We Live but How Much We Give

From one day to another
    God will gladly give
To everyone who seeks Him
    and tries each day to live
A little bit more closely
    to God and to each other,
Seeing everyone who passes
    as a neighbor, friend, or brother,
Not only joy and happiness
    but the faith to meet each trial
Not with fear and trepidation
    but with an "inner smile"—
For we know life's never measured
    by how many years we live
But by the kindly things we do
    and the happiness we give.

After the Winter . . . God Sends the Spring

Springtime is a season
        Of hope and joy and cheer.
There's beauty all around us
        To see and touch and hear . . .
So, no matter how downhearted
        And discouraged we may be,
New hope is born when we behold
        Leaves budding on a tree . . .
Or when we see a timid flower
        Push through the frozen sod
And open wide in glad surprise
        Its petaled eyes to God . . .
For this is just God saying,
        "Lift up your eyes to Me,
And the bleakness of your spirit,
        Like the budding springtime tree,
Will lose its wintry darkness
        And your heavy heart will sing"—
For God never sends the Winter
        Without the joy of Spring.

Spring Song

"The earth is the Lord's
        and the fulness thereof"—
It speaks of His greatness
        and it sings of His love,
And the wonder and glory
        of the first Easter morn,
Like the first Christmas night
        when the Saviour was born,
Are blended together
        in symphonic splendor
And God with a voice
        that is gentle and tender
Speaks to all hearts
        attuned to His voice,
Bidding His listeners
        to gladly rejoice . . .
For He who was born
        to be crucified
Arose from the grave
        to be glorified . . .
And the birds in the trees
        and the flowers of Spring
All join in proclaiming
        this heavenly King.

69

Showers of Blessings

Each day
there are showers of blessings
sent from the Father above,
For God is a great, lavish giver
and there is no end to His love—
His grace
is more than sufficient,
His mercy is boundless and deep,
and His infinite blessings
are countless
and all this we're given to keep,
If we but seek God
and find Him
and ask for a bounteous measure
Of this wholly immeasurable offering
from God's inexhaustible treasure—
For no matter
how big man's dreams are,
God's blessings are infinitely more,
For always God's giving
is greater
than what man is asking for.

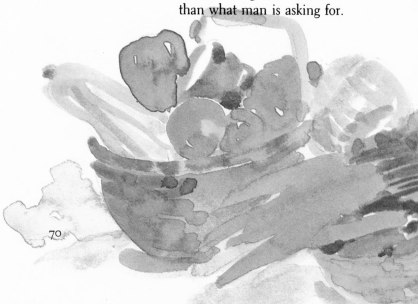

There's Sunshine in a Smile

Life is a mixture
    of sunshine and rain,
Laughter and pleasure,
    teardrops and pain,
All days can't be bright,
    but it's certainly true,
There was never a cloud
    the sun didn't shine through—
So just keep on smiling
    whatever betide you,
Secure in the knowledge
    God is always beside you,
And you'll find when you smile
    your day will be brighter
And all of your burdens
    will seem so much lighter—
For each time you smile
    you will find it is true
Somebody, somewhere
    will *smile back at you,*
And nothing on earth
    can make life more worthwhile
Than the sunshine and warmth
    of a *beautiful smile.*

Count Your Gains and Not Your Losses

As we travel down life's busy road
Complaining of our heavy load,
We often think God's been unfair
And gave us much more than our share
Of little daily irritations
And disappointing tribulations . . .

We're discontented with our lot
And all the "bad breaks" that we got,
We count our losses, not our gain,
And remember only tears and pain . . .
The good things we forget completely
When God looked down and blessed us sweetly,
Our troubles fill our every thought,
We dwell upon lost goals we sought,
And wrapped up in our own despair
We have no time to see or share
Another's load that far outweighs
Our little problems and dismays . . .
And so we walk with head held low
And little do we guess or know
That someone near us on life's street
Is burdened deeply with defeat . . .
But if we'd but forget *our care*
And stop in sympathy to share
The burden that "our brother" carried,
Our mind and heart would be less harried
And we would feel our load was small,
In fact, *we carried no load at all*.

"Flowers Leave Their Fragrance on the Hand That Bestows Them"

There's an old Chinese proverb,
    that, if practiced each day,
Would change the whole world
    in a wonderful way—
Its truth is so simple,
    it's so easy to do,
And it works every time
    and successfully, too—
For you can't do a kindness
    without a reward,
Not in silver nor gold
    but in joy from the Lord—
You can't light a candle
    to show others the way
Without feeling the warmth
    of that bright little ray—
And you can't pluck a rose,
    all fragrant with dew,
Without part of its fragrance
    remaining with you . . .
And whose hands bestow
    more fragrant bouquets
Than Mother who daily
    speaks kind words of praise,
A Mother whose courage
    and comfort and cheer
Lights bright little candles
    in hearts through the year—
No wonder the hands
    of an unselfish Mother
Are symbols of sweetness
    unlike any other.

Thank You, God, for Everything

Thank You, God, for everything—
    the big things and the small,
For "every good gift comes from God"—
    the Giver of them all—
And all too often we accept
    without any thanks or praise
The gifts God sends as blessings
    each day in many ways,
And so at this *Thanksgiving time*
    we offer up a prayer
To thank You, God, for giving us
    a lot more than our share . . .
First, thank You for the little things
    that often come our way,
The things we take for granted
    but don't mention when we pray,
The unexpected courtesy,
    The thoughtful, kindly deed,
A hand reached out to help us
    in the time of sudden need . . .
Oh, make us more aware, dear God,
    of little daily graces
That come to us with sweet surprise
    from never-dreamed-of places—
Then, thank You for the *miracles*
    we are much too blind to see,
And give us new awareness
    of our many gifts from Thee,
And help us to remember
    that the *key* to *life* and *living*
Is to make each prayer a *prayer of thanks*
    and every day *Thanksgiving*.

A Thankful Heart

Take nothing for granted,
      for whenever you do
The "joy of enjoying"
      is lessened for you—
For we rob our own lives
      much more than we know
When we fail to respond
      or in any way show
Our thanks for the blessings
      that daily are ours . . .
The warmth of the sun,
      the fragrance of flowers,
The beauty of twilight,
      the freshness of dawn,
The coolness of dew
      on a green velvet lawn,

The kind little deeds
        so thoughtfully done,
The favors of friends
        and the love that someone
Unselfishly gives us
        in a myriad of ways,
Expecting no payment
        and no words of praise—
Oh, great is our loss
        when we no longer find
A thankful response
        to things of this kind,
For the *joy of enjoying*
        and the *fulness of living*
Are found in the heart
        that is filled with *Thanksgiving.*

A Prayer of Thanks

Thank You, God, for everything
       I've experienced here on earth—
Thank You for protecting me
       from the moment of my birth—
And thank You for the beauty
       around me everywhere,
The gentle rain and glistening dew,
       the sunshine and the air,
The joyous gift of "feeling"
       the soul's soft, whispering voice
That speaks to me from deep within
       and makes my heart rejoice—
Oh, God, no words are great enough
       to thank You for just living,
And that is why every day
       is a day for real *Thanksgiving*.

Things to Be Thankful For

The good, green earth beneath our feet,
The air we breathe, the food we eat,
Some work to do, a goal to win,
A hidden longing deep within
That spurs us on to bigger things
And helps us meet what each day brings,
All these things and many more
Are things we should be thankful for . . .
And most of all our thankful prayers
Should rise to God because He cares!

Ideals Are Like Stars

In this world of casual carelessness
it's discouraging to try
To keep our morals and standards
and our ideals high . . .
We are ridiculed and laughed at
by the smart sophisticate
Who proclaims in brittle banter
that such things are
out of date . . .
But no life is worth the living
unless it's built on truth,
And we lay our life's foundation
in the golden years of youth . . .
So allow no one to stop you
or hinder you from laying
A firm and strong foundation
made of faith and love
and praying . . .
And remember that ideals
are like stars up in the sky,
You can never really reach them,
hanging in the heavens high . . .
But like the mighty mariner
who sailed the storm-tossed sea,
And used the stars to chart
his course
with skill and certainty,
You too can chart your course in life
With high ideals and love,
For high ideals are like the stars
that light the sky above . . .

You cannot ever
reach them,
but lift your heart up high
and your life will be as shining
as the stars up in the sky.

A Favorite Recipe

Take a cup of *kindness*, mix it well with *love*,
Add a lot of *patience* and *faith* in *God above*,
Sprinkle very generously with *joy* and *thanks* and *cheer*—
And you'll have lots of *"angel food"* to feast on all the
year.

"Climb Till Your Dream Comes True"

Often your tasks will be many,
And more than you think you can do . . .
Often the road will be rugged
And the hills insurmountable, too . . .
But always remember,
the hills ahead
Are never as steep as they seem,
And with faith in your heart
start upward
And climb till you reach your dream,
For nothing in life that is worthy
Is ever too hard to achieve
If you have the courage to try it
And you have the faith to believe . . .
For faith is a force that is greater
Than knowledge or power
or skill

And many defeats turn to triumph
If you trust in God's wisdom and will . . .
For faith is a mover of mountains,
There's nothing that God cannot do,
So start out today
with faith in your heart
And "Climb Till Your Dream Comes True"!

No Other Love Like Mother's Love

A Mother's love is something
  that no one can explain,
It is made of deep devotion
  and of sacrifice and pain,
It is endless and unselfish
  and enduring come what may
For nothing can destroy it
  or take that love away.

It is patient and forgiving
        when all others are forsaking,
And it never fails or falters
        even though the heart is breaking.
It believes beyond believing
        when the world around condemns,
And it glows with all the beauty
        of the rarest, brightest gems.
It is far beyond defining,
        it defies all explanation,
And it still remains a secret
        like the mysteries of creation.
A many-splendored miracle
        man cannot understand
And another wondrous evidence
        of God's tender guiding hand.

Fathers Are Wonderful People

Fathers are wonderful people
    too little understood,
And we do not sing their praises
    as often as we should,
For, somehow, Father seems to be
    the man who pays the bills,
While Mother binds up little hurts
    and nurses all our ills.
And Father struggles daily
    to live up to *"his image"*
As protector and provider
    and "hero of the scrimmage,"
And perhaps that is the reason
    we sometimes get the notion
That Fathers are not subject
    to the thing we call emotion,
But if you look inside Dad's heart,
    where no one else can see,
You'll find he's sentimental
    and as "soft" as he can be.
But he's so busy every day
    in the grueling race of life,
He leaves the sentimental stuff
    to his partner and his wife.
But Fathers are just *wonderful*
    in a million different ways,
And they merit loving compliments
    and accolades of praise,
For the only reason Dad aspires
    to fortune and success
Is to make the family proud of him
    and to bring them happiness.
And like *our heavenly Father,*
    he's a guardian and a guide,
Someone that we can count on
    to be *always on our side.*

89

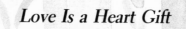

Love Is a Heart Gift

Love is a Heart Gift
    that cannot be bought or sold
For any amount
    of silver or gold . . .
And there could never be another
    who loves more deeply than a Mother!

Everyone Needs Someone

People need people and friends need friends,
And we all need love for a full life depends
Not on vast riches or great acclaim,
Not on success or on worldly fame,
But just in knowing that someone cares
And holds us close in their thoughts and prayers—
For only the knowledge that we're understood
Makes everyday living feel *wonderfully good*,
And we rob ourselves of life's greatest need
When we "lock up our hearts" and fail to heed
The outstretched hand reaching to find
A kindred spirit whose heart and mind
Are lonely and longing to somehow share
Our joys and sorrows and to make us aware
That life's completeness and richness depends
On the things we share with our loved ones and friends.

A Tribute to All Daughters

Every home should have a daughter,
      for there's nothing like a girl
To keep the world around her
      in one continuous whirl.
From the moment she arrives on earth,
      and on through womanhood,
A daughter is a *female*
      who is seldom understood.
One minute she is laughing,
      the next she starts to cry,

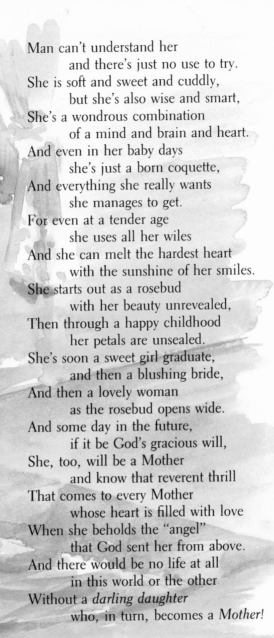

Man can't understand her
    and there's just no use to try.
She is soft and sweet and cuddly,
    but she's also wise and smart,
She's a wondrous combination
    of a mind and brain and heart.
And even in her baby days
    she's just a born coquette,
And everything she really wants
    she manages to get.
For even at a tender age
    she uses all her wiles
And she can melt the hardest heart
    with the sunshine of her smiles.
She starts out as a rosebud
    with her beauty unrevealed,
Then through a happy childhood
    her petals are unsealed.
She's soon a sweet girl graduate,
    and then a blushing bride,
And then a lovely woman
    as the rosebud opens wide.
And some day in the future,
    if it be God's gracious will,
She, too, will be a Mother
    and know that reverent thrill
That comes to every Mother
    whose heart is filled with love
When she beholds the "angel"
    that God sent her from above.
And there would be no life at all
    in this world or the other
Without a *darling daughter*
    who, in turn, becomes a *Mother!*

A Prayer for the Young and Lovely

Dear God, I keep praying
For the things I desire,
You tell me I'm selfish
And "playing with fire"
It is hard to believe
I am selfish and vain,
My desires seem so real
And my needs seem so sane,
And yet You are wiser
And Your vision is wide
And You look down on me
And You see deep inside,
You know it's so easy
To change and distort,
And things that are evil
Seem so harmless a sport
Oh, teach me, dear God,
To not rush ahead
But to pray for Your guidance
And to trust You instead,
For You know what I need
And that I'm only a slave
To the things that I want
And desire and crave

Oh, God, in your mercy
Look down on me now
And see in my heart
That I love you somehow,
Although in my rashness,
Impatience and greed
I pray for the things
That I *want* and *don't need*
And instead of a *crown*
Please send me a *cross*
And teach me to know
That *all gain* is but *loss*,
And show me the way
To joy without end,
With You as my *Father*,
Redeemer, and *Friend*
And send me the things
That are hardest to bear,
And keep me forever
Safe in Thy care.

Heart Gifts

It's not the things that can be bought
      that are life's richest treasure,
It's just the little "heart gifts"
      that money cannot measure . . .
A cheerful smile, a friendly word,
      a sympathetic nod
Are priceless little treasures
      from the storehouse of our God . . .
They are the things that can't be bought
      with silver or with gold,
For thoughtfulness and kindness
      and love are never sold . . .
They are the priceless things in life
      for which no one can pay
And the giver finds rich recompense
      in *giving them away.*